EAST INDIA
Publishing Company

SOCIALISM
John Stuart Mill

Published by the
EAST INDIA PUBLISHING COMPANY
Ottawa, Canada

Cover Design by EIPC © 2022
9781989201848

www.eastindiapublishing.com

CONTENTS

INTRODUCTORY

In the great country beyond the Atlantic, which is now well-nigh the most powerful country in the world, and will soon be indisputably so, manhood suffrage prevails. Such is also the political qualification of France since 1848, and has become that of the German Confederation, though not of all the several states composing it. In Great Britain the suffrage is not yet so widely extended, but the last Reform Act admitted within what is called the pale of the Constitution so large a body of those who live on weekly wages, that as soon and as often as these shall choose to act together as a class, and exert for any common object the whole of the electoral power which our present institutions give them, they will exercise, though not a complete ascendency, a very great influence on legislation. Now these are the very class which, in the vocabulary of the higher ranks, are said to have no stake in the country. Of course they have in reality the greatest stake, since their daily bread depends on its prosperity. But they are not engaged (we may call it bribed) by any peculiar interest of their own, to the support of property as it is, least of all to the support of inequalities of property. So far as their power reaches, or may hereafter reach, the laws of property have to depend for support upon considerations of a public nature, upon the estimate made of their conduciveness to the general welfare, and not upon motives of a mere personal character operating on the minds of those who have control over the Government.

It seems to me that the greatness of this change is as yet by no means completely realized, either by those who opposed, or by those who effected our last constitutional reform. To say the truth, the perceptions of Englishmen are of late somewhat blunted as to the tendencies of political changes. They have seen so many changes made, from which, while only in prospect, vast expectations were entertained, both of evil and of good, while the results of either kind that actually followed seemed far short of what had been predicted, that they have come to feel as if it were the nature of political changes not to fulfil expectation, and have fallen into a habit of half-unconscious belief that such changes, when they take place without a violent revolution, do not much or permanently disturb in practice the course of things habitual to the country. This, however, is but a superficial view either of the past or of the future. The various reforms of the last two generations have been at least as fruitful in important consequences as was foretold. The predictions were often erroneous as to the suddenness of the effects, and sometimes even as to the kind of effect. We laugh at the vain expectations of those who thought that Catholic emancipation would tranquilize Ireland, or reconcile it to British rule. At the end of the first ten years of the Reform Act of 1832, few continued to think either that it would remove every important practical grievance, or that it had opened the door to universal suffrage. But five-and-twenty years more of its operation had given scope for a large development of its indirect working, which is much more momentous than the direct. Sudden effects in history are generally superficial. Causes which go deep down into the roots of future events produce the most serious parts of their effect only slowly, and have, therefore, time to become a part of the familiar order of things before general attention is called to the changes they are producing; since, when the changes do become evident, they are often not seen, by cursory observers, to be in any peculiar manner connected with the cause. The remoter consequences of a new political fact are seldom understood when they occur, except when they have been appreciated beforehand.

This timely appreciation is particularly easy in respect to tendencies of the change made in our institutions by the Reform Act of 1867. The great increase of electoral power which the Act places within the reach of the working classes is permanent. The circumstances which have caused them, thus far, to make a very limited use of that power, are essentially temporary. It is known even to the most inobservant, that the working classes have, and are likely to have, political objects which concern them as working classes, and on which they believe, rightly or wrongly, that the interests and opinions of the other powerful classes are opposed to theirs. However much their pursuit of these objects may be for the present retarded by want of electoral organization, by dissensions among themselves, or by their not having reduced as yet their wishes into a sufficiently definite practical shape, it is as certain as anything in politics can be, that they will before long find the means of making their collective electoral power effectively instrumental to the proportion of their collective objects. And when they do so, it will not be in the disorderly and ineffective way which belongs to a people not habituated to the use of legal and constitutional machinery, nor will it be by the impulse of a mere instinct of levelling. The instruments will be the press, public meetings and associations, and the return to Parliament of the greatest possible number of persons pledged to the political aims of the working classes. The political aims will themselves be determined by definite political doctrines; for politics are now scientifically studied from the point of view of the working classes, and opinions conceived in the special interest of those classes are organized into systems and creeds which lay claim to a place on the platform of political philosophy, by the same right as the systems elaborated by previous thinkers. It is of the utmost importance that all reflecting persons should take into early consideration what these popular political creeds are likely to be, and that every single article of them should be brought under the fullest light of investigation and discussion, so that, if possible, when the time shall be ripe, whatever is right in them may be adopted, and what is wrong rejected by general consent, and that instead of a hostile conflict, physical or only moral, between the old and the new, the best parts of both may be combined in a renovated social fabric. At the ordinary pace of those great social changes which are not effected by physical violence, we have before us an interval of about a generation, on the due employment of which it depends whether the accommodation of social institutions to the altered state of human society, shall be the work of wise foresight, or of a conflict of opposite prejudices. The future of mankind will be gravely imperilled, if great questions are left to be fought over between ignorant change and ignorant opposition to change.

And the discussion that is now required is one that must go down to the very first principles of existing society. The fundamental doctrines which were assumed as incontestable by former generations, are now put again on

4

their trial. Until the present age, the institution of property in the shape in which it has been handed down from the past, had not, except by a few speculative writers, been brought seriously into question, because the conflicts of the past have always been conflicts between classes, both of which had a stake in the existing constitution of property. It will not be possible to go on longer in this manner. When the discussion includes classes who have next to no property of their own, and are only interested in the institution so far as it is a public benefit, they will not allow anything to be taken for granted—certainly not the principle of private property, the legitimacy and utility of which are denied by many of the reasoners who look out from the stand-point of the working classes. Those classes will certainly demand that the subject, in all its parts, shall be reconsidered from the foundation; that all proposals for doing without the institution, and all modes of modifying it which have the appearance of being favorable to the interest of the working classes, shall receive the fullest consideration and discussion before it is decided that the subject must remain as it is. As far as this country is concerned, the dispositions of the working classes have as yet manifested themselves hostile only to certain outlying portions of the proprietary system. Many of them desire to withdraw questions of wages from the freedom of contract, which is one of the ordinary attributions of private property. The more aspiring of them deny that land is a proper subject for private appropriation, and have commenced an agitation for its resumption by the State. With this is combined, in the speeches of some of the agitators, a denunciation of what they term usury, but without any definition of what they mean by the name; and the cry does not seem to be of home origin, but to have been caught up from the intercourse which has recently commenced through the Labor Congresses and the International Society, with the continental Socialists who object to all interest on money, and deny the legitimacy of deriving an income in any form from property apart from labor. This doctrine does not as yet show signs of being widely prevalent in Great Britain, but the soil is well prepared to receive the seeds of this description which are widely scattered from those foreign countries where large, general theories, and schemes of vast promise, instead of inspiring distrust, are essential to the popularity of a cause. It is in France, Germany, and Switzerland that anti-property doctrines in the widest sense have drawn large bodies of working men to rally round them. In these countries nearly all those who aim at reforming society in the interest of the working classes profess themselves Socialists, a designation under which schemes of very diverse character are comprehended and confounded, but which implies at least a remodelling generally approaching to abolition of the institution of private property. And it would probably be found that even in England the more prominent and active leaders of the working classes are usually in their private creed Socialists of one order or another, though being, like most English politicians, better aware than their Continental brethren that great and permanent changes in the fundamental ideas of mankind are not to be accomplished by a coup de main, they direct their practical efforts towards ends which seem within easier reach, and are content to hold back all extreme theories until there has been experience of the operation of the same principles on a partial scale. While such continues to be the character of the English working classes, as it is of Englishmen in general, they are not likely to rush head-long into the reckless extremities of some of the foreign Socialists, who, even in sober Switzerland, proclaim themselves content to begin by simple subversion, leaving the subsequent reconstruction to take care of itself; and by subversion, they mean not only the annihilation of all government, but getting all property of all kinds out of the hands of the possessors to be used for the general benefit; but in what mode it will, they say, be time enough afterwards to decide.

The avowal of this doctrine by a public newspaper, the organ of an association (La Solidarite published at Neuchatel), is one of the most curious signs of the times. The leaders of the English working-men—whose delegates at the congresses of Geneva and Bale contributed much the greatest part of such practical common sense as was shown there—are not likely to begin deliberately by anarchy, without having formed any opinion as to what form of society should be established in the room of the old. But it is evident that whatever they do propose can only be properly judged, and the grounds of the judgment made convincing to the general mind, on the basis of a previous survey of the two rival theories, that of private property and that of Socialism, one or other of which must necessarily furnish most of the premises in the discussion. Before, therefore, we can usefully discuss this class of questions in detail, it will be advisable to examine from their foundations the general question raised by Socialism. And this examination should be made without any hostile prejudice. However irrefutable the arguments in favor of the laws of property may appear to those to whom they have the double prestige of immemorial custom and of personal interest, nothing is more natural than that a working man who has begun to speculate on politics, should regard them in a very different light. Having, after long struggles, attained in some countries, and nearly attained in others, the point at which for them, at least, there is no further progress to make in the department of purely political rights, is it possible that the less fortunate classes among the "adult males" should not ask themselves whether progress ought to stop there? Notwithstanding all that has been done, and all that seems likely to be done, in the extension of franchises, a few are born to great riches, and the many to a penury, made only more grating by contrast. No longer enslaved or made dependent by force of law, the great majority are so by force of poverty; they are still chained to a place, to an occupation, and to conformity with the will of an employer, and debarred by the accident of birth both from the enjoyments, and from the mental and moral advantages, which others inherit without exertion and independently of desert. That this is an evil equal to almost any of those against which mankind have hitherto struggled, the poor are not wrong in believing. Is it a necessary evil? They are told so by those who do not feel it—by those who have gained the prizes in the lottery of life. But it was also said that slavery, that despotism, that all the privileges of oligarchy were necessary. All the successive steps that have been made by the poorer classes, partly won from the better feelings of the powerful, partly extorted from their fears, and partly bought with money, or attained in exchange for support given to one section of the powerful in its quarrels with another, had the strongest prejudices opposed to them beforehand; but their acquisition was a sign of power gained by the subordinate classes, a means to those classes of acquiring more; it consequently drew to those classes a certain share of the respect accorded to power, and produced a corresponding modification in the creed of society respecting them; whatever advantages they succeeded in acquiring came to be considered their due, while, of those which they had not yet attained, they continued to be deemed unworthy. The classes, therefore, which the system of society makes subordinate, have little reason to put faith in any of the maxims which the same system of society may have established as principles. Considering that the opinions of mankind have been found so wonderfully flexible, have always tended to consecrate existing facts, and to declare what did not yet exist, either pernicious or impracticable, what assurance have those classes that the distinction of rich and poor is grounded on a more imperative necessity than those other ancient and long-established facts, which, having been abolished, are now condemned even by those who formerly profited by them? This cannot be taken on the word of an interested party. The working classes are entitled to claim that the whole field of social institutions should be re-examined, and every question considered as if it now arose for the first time; with the idea constantly in view that the persons who are to be convinced are not those who owe their ease and importance to the present system, but persons who have no other interest in the matter than abstract justice and the general good of the community. It should be the object to ascertain what institutions of property would be established by an unprejudiced legislator, absolutely impartial between the possessors of property and the non-possessors; and to defend and to justify them by the reasons which would really influence such a legislator, and not by such as have the appearance of being got up to make out a case for what already exists. Such rights or privileges of property as will not stand this test will, sooner or later, have to be given up. An impartial hearing ought, moreover, to be given to all objections against property itself. All evils and inconveniences attaching to the institution in its best form ought to be frankly admitted, and the best remedies or palliatives applied which human intelligence is able to devise. And all plans proposed by social reformers, under whatever name designated, for the purpose of attaining the benefits aimed at by the institution of property without its inconveniences, should be examined with the same candor, not prejudged as absurd or impracticable.

SOCIALIST OBJECTIONS TO THE
PRESENT ORDER OF SOCIETY

As in all proposals for change there are two elements to be considered—that which is to be changed, and that which it is to be changed to—so in Socialism considered generally, and in each of its varieties taken separately, there are two parts to be distinguished, the one negative and critical, the other constructive. There is, first, the judgment of Socialism on existing institutions and practices and on their results; and secondly, the various plans which it has propounded for doing better. In the former all the different schools of Socialism are at one. They agree almost to identity in the faults which they find with the economical order of existing society. Up to a certain point also they entertain the same general conception of the remedy to be provided for those faults; but in the details, notwithstanding this general agreement, there is a wide disparity. It will be both natural and convenient, in attempting an estimate of their doctrines, to begin with the negative portion which is common to them all, and to postpone all mention of their differences until we arrive at that second part of their undertaking, in which alone they seriously differ.

This first part of our task is by no means difficult; since it consists only in an enumeration of existing evils. Of these there is no scarcity, and most of them are by no means obscure or mysterious. Many of them are the veriest commonplaces of moralists, though the roots

11

even of these lie deeper than moralists usually attempt to penetrate. So various are they that the only difficulty is to make any approach to an exhaustive catalogue. We shall content ourselves for the present with mentioning a few of the principal. And let one thing be remembered by the reader. When item after item of the enumeration passes before him, and he finds one fact after another which he has been accustomed to include among the necessities of nature urged as an accusation against social institutions, he is not entitled to cry unfairness, and to protest that the evils complained of are inherent in Man and Society, and are such as no arrangements can remedy. To assert this would be to beg the very question at issue. No one is more ready than Socialists to admit—they affirm it indeed much more decidedly than truth warrants—that the evils they complain of are irremediable in the present constitution of society. They propose to consider whether some other form of society may be devised which would not be liable to those evils, or would be liable to them in a much less degree. Those who object to the present order of society, considered as a whole and who accept as an alternative the possibility of a total change, have a right to set down all the evils which at present exist in society as part of their case, whether these are apparently attributable to social arrangements or not, provided they do not flow from physical laws which human power is not adequate, or human knowledge has not yet learned, to counteract. Moral evils and such physical evils as would be remedied if all persons did as they ought, are fairly chargeable against the state of society which admits of them; and are valid as arguments until it is shown that any other state of society would involve an equal or greater amount of such evils. In the opinion of Socialists, the present arrangements of society in respect to Property and the Production and Distribution of Wealth, are as means to the general good, a total failure. They say that there is an enormous mass of evil which these arrangements do not succeed in preventing; that the good, either moral or physical, which they realize is wretchedly small compared with the amount of exertion employed, and that even this small amount of good is brought about by means which are full of pernicious consequences, moral and physical.

First among existing social evils may be mentioned the evil of Poverty. The institution of Property is upheld and commended principally as being the means by which labor and frugality are insured their reward, and mankind enabled to emerge from indigence. It may be so; most Socialists allow that it has been so in earlier periods of history. But if the institution can do nothing more or better in this respect than it has hitherto done, its capabilities, they affirm, are very insignificant. What proportion of the population, in the most civilized countries of Europe, enjoy in their own persons anything worth naming of the benefits of property? It may be said, that but for property in the hands of their employers they would be without daily bread; but, though this be conceded, at least their daily bread is all that they have; and that often in insufficient quantity; almost always of inferior quality; and with no assurance of continuing to have it at all; an immense proportion of the industrious classes being at some period or other of their lives (and all being liable to become) dependent, at least temporarily, on legal or voluntary charity. Any attempt to depict the miseries of indigence, or to estimate the proportion of mankind who in the most advanced countries are habitually given up during their whole existence to its physical and moral sufferings, would be superfluous here. This may be left to philanthropists, who have painted these miseries in colors sufficiently strong. Suffice it to say that the condition of numbers in civilized Europe, and even in England and France, is more wretched than that of most tribes of savages who are known to us.

It may be said that of this hard lot no one has any reason to complain, because it befalls those only who are outstripped by others, from inferiority of energy or of prudence. This, even were it true, would be a very small alleviation of the evil. If some Nero or Domitian was to require a hundred persons to run a race for their lives, on condition that the fifty or twenty who came in hindmost should be put to death, it would not be any diminution of the injustice that the strongest or nimblest would, except through some untoward accident, be certain to escape. The misery and the crime would be that they were put to death at all. So in the economy of society; if there be any who suffer physical privation or moral degradation, whose bodily necessities are either not satisfied or satisfied in a manner which only brutish creatures can be content with, this, though not necessarily the crime of society, is pro tanto a failure of the social arrangements. And to assert as a mitigation of the evil that those who thus suffer are the weaker members of the community, morally or physically, is to add insult to misfortune. Is weakness a justification of suffering? Is it not, on the contrary, an irresistible claim upon every human being for protection against suffering? If the minds and feelings of the prosperous were in a right state, would they accept their prosperity if for the sake of it even one person near them was, for any other cause than voluntary fault, excluded from obtaining a desirable existence?

One thing there is, which if it could be affirmed truly, would relieve social institutions from any share in the responsibility of these evils. Since the human race has no means of enjoyable existence, or of existence at all, but what it derives from its own labor and abstinence, there would be no ground for complaint against society if every one who was willing to undergo a fair share of this labor and abstinence could attain a fair share of the fruits. But is this the fact? Is it not the reverse of the fact? The reward, instead of being proportioned to the labor and abstinence of the individual, is almost in an inverse ratio to it: those who receive the least, labor and abstain the most. Even the idle, reckless, and ill-conducted poor, those who are said with most justice to have themselves to blame for their condition, often undergo much more and severer labor, not only than those who are born to pecuniary independence, but than almost any of the more highly remunerated of those who earn their subsistence; and even the inadequate self-control exercised by the industrious poor costs them more sacrifice and more effort than is almost ever required from the more favored members of society. The very idea of distributive justice, or of any proportionality between success and merit, or between success and exertion, is in the present state of society so manifestly chimerical as to be relegated to the regions of romance. It is true that the lot of individuals is not wholly independent of their virtue and intelligence; these do really tell in their favor, but far less than many other things in which there is no merit at all. The most powerful of all the determining circumstances is birth. The great majority are what they were born to be. Some are born rich without work, others are born to a position in which they can become rich by work, the great majority are born to hard work and poverty throughout life, numbers to indigence. Next to birth the chief cause of success in life is accident and opportunity. When a person not born to riches succeeds in acquiring them, his own industry and dexterity have generally contributed to the result; but industry and dexterity would not have sufficed unless there had been also a concurrence of occasions and chances which falls to the lot of only a small number. If persons are helped in their worldly career by their virtues, so are they, and perhaps quite as often, by their vices: by servility and sycophancy, by hard-hearted and close-fisted selfishness, by the permitted lies and tricks of trade, by gambling speculations, not seldom by downright knavery. Energies and talents are of much more avail for success in life than virtues; but if one man succeeds by employing energy and talent in something generally useful, another thrives by exercising the same qualities in out-generalling and ruining a rival. It is as much as any moralist ventures to assert, that, other circumstances being given, honesty is the best policy, and that with parity of advantages an honest person has a better chance than a rogue. Even this in many stations and circumstances of life is questionable; anything more than this is out of the question. It cannot be pretended that honesty, as a means of success, tells for as much as a difference of one single step on the social ladder. The connection between fortune and conduct is mainly this, that there is a degree of bad conduct, or rather of some kinds of bad conduct, which suffices to ruin any amount of good fortune; but the converse is not true: in the situation of most people no degree whatever of good conduct can be counted upon for raising them in the world, without the aid of fortunate accidents.

These evils, then—great poverty, and that poverty very little connected with desert—are the first grand failure of the existing arrangements of society. The second is human misconduct; crime, vice, and folly, with all the sufferings which follow in their train. For, nearly all the forms of misconduct, whether committed towards ourselves or towards others, may be traced to one of three causes: Poverty and its temptations in the many; Idleness and desœuvrement in the few whose circumstances do not compel them to work; bad education, or want of education, in both. The first two must be allowed to be at least failures in the social arrangements, the last is now almost universally admitted to be the fault of those arrangements—it may almost be said the crime. I am speaking loosely and in the rough, for a minuter analysis of the sources of faults of character and errors of conduct would establish far more conclusively the filiation which connects them with a defective organization of society, though it would also show the reciprocal dependence of that faulty state of society on a backward state of the human mind.

At this point, in the enumeration of the evils of society, the mere levellers of former times usually stopped; but their more far-sighted successors, the present Socialists, go farther. In their eyes the very foundation of human life as at present constituted, the very principle on which the production and repartition of all material products is now carried on, is essentially vicious and anti-social. It is the principle of individualism, competition, each one for himself and against all the rest. It is grounded on opposition of interests, not harmony of interests, and under it every one is required to find his place by a struggle, by pushing others back or being pushed back by them. Socialists consider this system of private war (as it may be termed) between every one and every one, especially

17

fatal in an economical point of view and in a moral. Morally considered, its evils are obvious. It is the parent of envy, hatred, and all uncharitableness; it makes every one the natural enemy of all others who cross his path, and every one's path is constantly liable to be crossed. Under the present system hardly any one can gain except by the loss or disappointment of one or of many others. In a well-constituted community every one would be a gainer by every other person's successful exertions; while now we gain by each other's loss and lose by each other's gain, and our greatest gains come from the worst source of all, from death, the death of those who are nearest and should be dearest to us. In its purely economical operation the principle of individual competition receives as unqualified condemnation from the social reformers as in its moral. In the competition of laborers they see the cause of low wages; in the competition of producers the cause of ruin and bankruptcy; and both evils, they affirm, tend constantly to increase as population and wealth make progress; no person (they conceive) being benefited except the great proprietors of land, the holders of fixed money incomes, and a few great capitalists, whose wealth is gradually enabling them to undersell all other producers, to absorb the whole of the operations of industry into their own sphere, to drive from the market all employers of labor except themselves, and to convert the laborers into a kind of slaves or serfs, dependent on them for the means of support, and compelled to accept these on such terms as they choose to offer. Society, in short, is travelling onward, according to these speculators, towards a new feudality, that of the great capitalists.

As I shall have ample opportunity in future chapters to state my own opinion on these topics, and on many others connected with and subordinate to them, I shall now, without further preamble, exhibit the opinions of distinguished Socialists on the present arrangements of society, in a selection of passages from their published writings. For the present I desire to be considered as a mere reporter of the opinions of others. Hereafter it will appear how much of what I cite agrees or differs with my own sentiments.

The clearest, the most compact, and the most precise and specific statement of the case of the Socialists generally against the existing order of society in the economical department of human affairs, is to be found in the little work of M. Louis Blanc, Organisation du Travail. My first extracts, therefore, on this part of the subject, shall be taken from that treatise.

"Competition is for the people a system of extermination. Is the poor man a member of society, or an enemy to it? We ask for an answer.

"All around him he finds the soil preoccupied. Can he cultivate the earth for himself? No; for the right of the first occupant has become a right of property. Can he gather the fruits which the hand of God ripens on the path of man? No; for, like the soil, the fruits have been appropriated. Can he hunt or fish? No; for that is a right which is dependent upon the government. Can he draw water from a spring enclosed in a field? No; for the proprietor of the field is, in virtue of his right to the field, proprietor of the fountain. Can he, dying of hunger and thirst, stretch out his hands for the charity of his fellow-creatures? No; for there are laws against begging. Can he, exhausted by fatigue and without a refuge, lie down to sleep upon the pavement of the streets? No; for there are laws against vagabondage. Can he, dying from the cruel native land where everything is denied him, seek the means of living far from the place where life was given him? No; for it is not permitted to change your country except on certain conditions which the poor man cannot fulfil.

"What, then, can the unhappy man do? He will say, 'I have hands to work with, I have intelligence, I have youth, I have strength; take all this, and in return give me a morsel of bread.' This is what the working-men do say. But even here the poor man may be answered, 'I have no work to give you.' What is he to do then?"

"What is competition from the point of view of the workman? It is work put up to auction. A contractor wants a workman: three present themselves.—How much for your work?—Half-a-crown; I have a wife and children.—Well; and how much for yours?—Two shillings: I have no children, but I have a wife.—Very well; and now how much for you?—One and eightpence are enough for me; I am single. Then you shall have the work. It is done; the bargain is struck. And what are the other two workmen to do? It is to be hoped they will die quietly of hunger. But what if they take to thieving? Never fear; we have the police. To murder? We have got the hangman. As for the lucky one, his triumph is only temporary. Let a fourth workman make his appearance, strong enough to fast every other day, and his price will run down still lower; then there will be a new outcast, a new recruit for the prison perhaps!

"Will it be said that these melancholy results are exaggerated; that at all events they are only possible when there is not work enough for the hands that seek

20

employment? But I ask, in answer, Does the principle of competition contain, by chance, within itself any method by which this murderous disproportion is to be avoided? If one branch of industry is in want of hands, who can answer for it that, in the confusion created by universal competition, another is not overstocked? And if, out of thirty-four millions of men, twenty are really reduced to theft for a living, this would suffice to condemn the principle.

"But who is so blind as not to see that under the system of unlimited competition, the continual fall of wages is no exceptional circumstance, but a necessary and general fact? Has the population a limit which it cannot exceed? Is it possible for us to say to industry—industry given up to the accidents of individual egotism and fertile in ruin—can we say, 'Thus far shalt thou go, and no farther?' The population increases constantly: tell the poor mother to become sterile, and blaspheme the God who made her fruitful, for if you do not, the lists will soon become too narrow for the combatants. A machine is invented: command it to be broken, and anathematize science, for if you do not, the thousand workmen whom the new machine deprives of work will knock at the door of the neighboring workshop, and lower the wages of their companions. Thus systematic lowering of wages, ending in the driving out of a certain number of workmen, is the inevitable effect of unlimited competition. It is an industrial system by means of which the working-classes are forced to exterminate one another."

"If there is an undoubted fact, it is that the increase of population is much more rapid among the poor than among the rich. According to the Statistics of European Population, the births at Paris are only one-thirty-second of the population in the rich quarters, while in the others they rise to one-twenty-sixth. This disproportion is a general fact, and M. de Sismondi, in his work on Political Economy, has explained it by the impossibility for the workmen of hopeful prudence. Those only who feel themselves assured of the morrow can regulate the number of their children according to their income; he who lives from day to day is under the yoke of a mysterious fatality, to which he sacrifices his children as he was sacrificed to it himself. It is true the workhouses exist, menacing society with an inundation of beggars—what way is there of escaping from the cause?... It is clear that any society where the means of subsistence increase less rapidly than the numbers of the population, is a society on the brink of an abyss.... Competition produces destitution; this is a fact shown by statistics. Destitution is fearfully prolific; this is shown by statistics. The fruitfulness of the poor throws upon society unhappy creatures who have need of work and cannot find it; this is shown by statistics. At this point society is reduced to a choice between killing the poor or maintaining them gratuitously—between atrocity or folly."

So much for the poor. We now pass to the middle classes.

"According to the political economists of the school of Adam Smith and Leon Say, cheapness is the word in which may be summed up the advantages of unlimited competition. But why persist in considering the effect of cheapness with a view only to the momentary advantage of the consumer? Cheapness is advantageous to the consumer at the cost of introducing the seeds of ruinous anarchy among the producers. Cheapness is, so to speak, the hammer with which the rich among the producers crush their poorer rivals. Cheapness is the trap into which the daring speculators entice the hard-workers. Cheapness is the sentence of death to the producer on a small scale who has no money to invest in the purchase of machinery that his rich rivals can easily procure. Cheapness is the great instrument in the hands of monopoly; it absorbs the small manufacturer, the small shopkeeper, the small proprietor; it is, in one word, the destruction of the middle classes for the advantage of a few industrial oligarchs.

"Ought we, then, to consider cheapness as a curse? No one would attempt to maintain such an absurdity. But it is the specialty of wrong principles to turn good into evil and to corrupt all things. Under the system of competition cheapness is only a provisional and fallacious advantage. It is maintained only so long as there is a struggle; no sooner have the rich competitors driven out their poorer rivals than prices rise. Competition leads to monopoly, for the same reason cheapness leads to high prices. Thus, what has been made use of as a weapon in the contest between the producers, sooner or later becomes a cause of impoverishment among the consumers. And if to this cause we add the others we have already enumerated, first among which must be ranked the inordinate increase of the population, we shall be compelled to recognize the impoverishment of the mass of the consumers as a direct consequence of competition.

"But, on the other hand, this very competition which tends to dry up the sources of demand, urges production to over-supply. The confusion produced by the universal struggle prevents each producer from knowing the state of the market. He must work in the dark, and trust to chance for a sale. Why should he check the supply, especially as he can throw any loss on the workman whose wages are so pre-eminently liable to rise and fall? Even when production is carried on at a loss the manufacturers still often carry it on, because they will not let their machinery, &c., stand idle, or risk the loss of raw material, or lose their customers; and because productive industry as carried on under the competitive system being nothing else than a game of chance, the gambler will not lose his chance of a lucky stroke.

"Thus, and we cannot too often insist upon it, competition necessarily tends to increase supply and to diminish consumption; its tendency therefore is precisely the opposite of what is sought by economic science; hence it is not merely oppressive but foolish as well."

"And in all this, in order to avoid dwelling on truths which have become commonplaces, and sound declamatory from their very truth, we have said nothing of the frightful moral corruption which industry, organized, or more properly speaking, disorganized, as it is at the present day, has introduced among the middle classes. Everything has become venal, and competition invades even the domain of thought.

"The factory crushing the workshop; the showy establishment absorbing the humble shop; the artisan who is his own master replaced by the day-laborer; cultivation by the plow superseding that by the spade, and bringing the poor man's field under disgraceful homage to the money-lender; bankruptcies multiplied; manufacturing industry transformed by the ill-regulated extension of credit into a system of gambling where no one, not even the rogue, can be sure of winning; in short a vast confusion calculated to arouse jealousy, mistrust, and hatred, and to stifle, little by little, all generous aspirations, all faith, self-sacrifice, and poetry—such is the hideous but only too faithful picture of the results obtained by the application of the principle of competition."

The Fourierists, through their principal organ, M. Considérant, enumerate the evils of the existing civilisation in the following order:—

1. It employs an enormous quantity of labor and of human power unproductively, or in the work of destruction.

"In the first place there is the army, which in France, as in all other countries, absorbs the healthiest and strongest men, a large number of the most talented and intelligent, and a considerable part of the public revenue.... The existing state of society develops in its impure atmosphere innumerable outcasts, whose labor is not merely unproductive, but actually destructive: adventurers, prostitutes, people with no acknowledged means of living, beggars, convicts, swindlers, thieves, and others whose numbers tend rather to increase than to diminish....

"To the list of unproductive labor fostered by our state of Society must be added that of the judicature and of the bar, of the courts of law and magistrates, the police, jailers, executioners, &c.,—functions indispensable to the state of society as it is.

"Also people of what is called 'good society'; those who pass their lives in doing nothing; idlers of all ranks.

"Also the numberless custom-house officials, tax-gatherers, bailiffs, excise-men; in short, all that army of men which overlooks, brings to account, takes, but produces nothing.

"Also the labors of sophists, philosophers, metaphysicians, political men, working in mistaken directions, who do nothing to advance science, and produce nothing but disturbance and sterile discussions; the verbiage of advocates, pleaders, witnesses, &c.

"And finally all the operations of commerce, from those of the bankers and brokers, down to those of the grocer behind his counter."

Secondly, they assert that even the industry and powers which in the present system are devoted to production, do not produce more than a small portion of what they might produce if better employed and directed:—

"Who with any good-will and reflection will not see how much the want of coherence—the disorder, the want of combination, the parcelling out of labor and leaving it wholly to individual action without any organization, without any large or general views—are causes which limit the possibilities of production,

26

and destroy, or at least waste, our means of action? Does not disorder give birth to poverty, as order and good management give birth to riches? Is not want of combination a source of weakness, as combination is a source of strength? And who can say that industry, whether agricultural, domestic, manufacturing, scientific, artistic, or commercial, is organized at the present day either in the state or in municipalities? Who can say that all the work which is carried on in any of these departments is executed in subordination to any general views, or with foresight, economy, and order? Or, again, who can say that it is possible in our present state of society to develop, by a good education, all the faculties bestowed by nature on each of its members; to employ each one in functions which he would like, which he would be the most capable of, and which, therefore, he could carry on with the greatest advantage to himself and to others? Has it even been so much as attempted to solve the problems presented by varieties of character so as to regulate and harmonize the varieties of employments in accordance with natural aptitudes? Alas! The Utopia of the most ardent philanthropists is to teach reading and writing to twenty-five millions of the French people! And in the present state of things we may defy them to succeed even in that!

"And is it not a strange spectacle, too, and one which cries out in condemnation of us, to see this state of society where the soil is badly cultivated, and sometimes not cultivated at all; where man is ill lodged, ill clothed, and yet where whole masses are continually in need of work and pining in misery because they cannot find it? Of a truth we are forced to acknowledge that if the nations are poor and starving it is not because nature has denied the means of producing wealth, but because of the anarchy and disorder in our employment of those means; in other words, it is because society is wretchedly constituted and labor unorganized.

"But this is not all, and you will have but a faint conception of the evil if you do not consider that to all these vices of society, which dry up the sources of wealth and prosperity, must be added the struggle, the discord, the war, in short under many names and many forms which society cherishes and cultivates between the individuals that compose it. These struggles and discords correspond to radical oppositions—deep-seated antinomies between the various interests. Exactly in so far as you are able to establish classes and categories within the nation; in so far, also, you will have opposition of interests and internal warfare either avowed or secret, even if you take into consideration the industrial system only."

One of the leading ideas of this school is the wastefulness and at the same time the immorality of the existing arrangements for distributing the produce of the country among the various consumers, the enormous superfluity in point of number of the agents of distribution, the merchants, dealers, shopkeepers and their innumerable, employés, and the depraving character of such a distribution of occupations.

"It is evident that the interest of the trader is opposed to that of the consumer and of the producer. Has he not bought cheap and under-valued as much as possible in all his dealings with the producer, the very same article which, vaunting its excellence, he sells to you as dear as he can? Thus the interest of the commercial body, collectively and individually, is contrary to that of the producer and of the consumer—that is to say, to the interest of the whole body of society.

"The trader is a go-between, who profits by the general anarchy and the non-organization of industry. The trader buys up products, he buys up everything; he owns and detains everything, in such sort that:—

"1stly. He holds both Production and Consumption under his yoke, because both must come to him either finally for the products to be consumed, or at first for the raw materials to be worked up. Commerce with all its methods of buying, and of raising and lowering prices, its innumerable devices, and its holding everything in the hands of middle-men, levies toll right and left; it despotically gives the law to Production and Consumption, of which it ought to be only the subordinate.

"2ndly. It robs society by its enormous profits— profits levied upon the consumer and the producer, and altogether out of proportion to the services rendered, for which a twentieth of the persons actually employed would be sufficient.

"3rdly. It robs society by the subtraction of its productive forces; taking off from productive labor nineteen-twentieths of the agents of trade who are mere parasites. Thus, not only does commerce rob society by appropriating an exorbitant share of the common wealth, but also by considerably diminishing the productive energy of the human beehive. The great majority of traders would return to productive work if a rational system of commercial organization were substituted for the inextricable chaos of the present state of things.

"4thly. It robs society by the adulteration of products, pushed at the present day beyond all bounds. And in fact, if a hundred grocers establish themselves in a town where before there were only twenty, it is plain that people will not begin to consume five times as many groceries. Hereupon the hundred virtuous grocers have to dispute between them the profits which before were honestly made by the twenty; competition obliges them to make it up at the expense of the consumer, either by raising the prices as sometimes happens, or by adulterating the goods as always happens. In such a state of things there is an end to good faith. Inferior or adulterated goods are sold for articles of good quality whenever the credulous customer is not too experienced to be deceived. And when the customer has been thoroughly imposed upon, the trading conscience consoles itself by saying, 'I state my price; people can take or leave; no one is obliged to buy.' The losses imposed on the consumers by the bad quality or the adulteration of goods are incalculable.

"5thly. It robs society by accumulations, artificial or not, in consequence of which vast quantities of goods, collected in one place, are damaged and destroyed for want of a sale. Fourier (Th. des Quat. Mouv., p. 334, 1st ed.) says: 'The fundamental principle of the commercial systems, that of leaving full liberty to the merchants, gives them absolute right of property over the goods in which they deal: they have the right to withdraw them altogether, to withhold or even to burn them, as happened more than once with the Oriental Company of Amsterdam, which publicly burnt stores of cinnamon in order to raise the price. What it did with cinnamon it would have done with corn; but for the fear of being stoned by the populace, it would have burnt some corn in order to sell the rest at four times its value. Indeed, it actually is of daily occurrence in ports, for provisions of grains to be thrown into the sea because the merchants have allowed them to rot while waiting for a rise. I myself, when I was a clerk, have had to superintend these infamous proceedings, and in one day caused to be thrown into the sea some forty thousand bushels of rice, which might have been sold at a fair profit had the withholder been less greedy of gain. It is society that bears the cost of this waste, which takes place daily under shelter of the philosophical maxim of full liberty for the merchants.'

"6thly. Commerce robs society, moreover, by all the loss, damage, and waste that follows from the extreme scattering of products in millions of shops, and by the multiplication and complication of carriage.

"7thly. It robs society by shameless and unlimited usury—usury absolutely appalling. The trader carries on operations with fictitious capital, much higher in amount than his real capital. A trader with a capital of twelve hundred pounds will carry on operations, by means of bills and credit, on a scale of four, eight, or twelve thousand pounds. Thus he draws from capital which he does not possess, usurious interest, out of all proportion with the capital he actually owns.

"8thly. It robs society by innumerable bankruptcies, for the daily accidents of our commercial system, political events, and any kind of disturbance, must usher in a day when the trader, having incurred obligations beyond his means, is no longer able to meet them; his failure, whether fraudulent or not, must be a severe blow to his creditors. The bankruptcy of some entails that of others, so that bankruptcies follow one upon another, causing widespread ruin. And it is always the producer and the consumer who suffer; for commerce, considered as a whole, does not produce wealth, and invests very little in proportion to the wealth which passes through its hands. How many are the manufactures crushed by these blows! how many fertile sources of wealth dried up by these devices, with all their disastrous consequences!

"The producer furnishes the goods, the consumer the money. Trade furnishes credit, founded on little or no actual capital, and the different members of the commercial body are in no way responsible for one another. This, in a few words, is the whole theory of the thing.

"9thly. Commerce robs society by the independence and irresponsibility which permits it to buy at the epochs when the producers are forced to sell and compete with one another, in order to procure money for their rent and necessary expenses of production. When the markets are overstocked and goods cheap, trade purchases. Then it creates a rise, and by this simple manœuvre despoils both producer and consumer.

"10thly. It robs society by a considerable drawing off of capital, which will return to productive industry when commerce plays its proper subordinate part, and is only an agency carrying on transactions between the producers (more or less distant) and the great centres of consumption—the communistic societies. Thus the capital engaged in the speculations of commerce (which, small as it is, compared to the immense wealth which passes through its hands, consists nevertheless of sums enormous in themselves), would return to stimulate production if commerce was deprived of the intermediate property in goods, and their distribution became a matter of administrative organization. Stock-jobbing is the most odious form of this vice of commerce.

"11thly. It robs society by the monopolising or buying up of raw materials. 'For' (says Fourier, Th. des Quat. Mouv., p. 359, 1st ed.), 'the rise in price on articles that are bought up, is borne ultimately by the consumer, although in the first place by the manufacturers, who, being obliged to keep up their establishments, must make pecuniary sacrifices, and manufacture at small profits in the hope of better days; and it is often long before they can repay themselves the rise in prices which the monopoliser has compelled them to support in the first instance...."

"In short, all these vices, besides many others which I omit, are multiplied by the extreme complication of mercantile affairs; for products do not pass once only through the greedy clutches of commerce; there are some which pass and repass twenty or thirty times before reaching the consumer. In the first place, the raw material passes through the grasp of commerce before reaching the manufacturer who first works it up; then it returns to commerce to be sent out again to be worked up in a second form; and so on until it receives its final shape. Then it passes into the hands of merchants, who sell to the wholesale dealers, and these to the great retail dealers of towns, and these again to the little dealers and to the country shops; and each time that it changes hands, it leaves something behind it.

"... One of my friends who was lately exploring the Jura, where much working in metal is done, had occasion to enter the house of a peasant who was a manufacturer of shovels. He asked the price. 'Let us come to an understanding,' answered the poor laborer, not an economist at all, but a man of common sense; 'I sell them for 8d. to the trade, which retails them at 1s. 8d. in the towns. If you could find a means of opening a direct communication between the workman and the consumer, you might have them for 1s. 2d., and we should each gain 6d. by the transaction.'"

To a similar effect Owen, in the Book of the New Moral World, part 2, chap. iii.

"The principle now in practice is to induce a large portion of society to devote their lives to distribute wealth upon a large, a medium, and a small scale, and to have it conveyed from place to place in larger or smaller quantities, to meet the means and wants of various divisions of society and individuals, as they are now situated in cities, towns, villages, and country places. This principle of distribution makes a class in society whose business is to buy from some parties and to sell to others. By this proceeding they are placed under circumstances which induce them to endeavor to buy at what appears at the time a low price in the market, and to sell again at the greatest permanent profit which they can obtain. Their real object being to get as much profit as gain between the seller to, and the buyer from them, as can be effected in their transactions.

"There are innumerable errors in principle and evils in practice which necessarily proceed from this mode of distributing the wealth of society.

"1st. A general class of distributers is formed, whose interest is separated from, and apparently opposed to, that of the individual from whom they buy and to whom they sell.

"2nd. Three classes of distributers are made, the small, the medium, and the large buyers and sellers; or the retailers, the wholesale dealers, and the extensive merchants.

"3rd. Three classes of buyers thus created constitute the small, the medium, and the large purchasers.

"By this arrangement into various classes of buyers and sellers, the parties are easily trained to learn that they have separate and opposing interests, and different ranks and stations in society. An inequality of feeling and condition is thus created and maintained, with all the servility and pride which these unequal arrangements are sure to produce. The parties are regularly trained in a general system of deception, in order that they may be the more successful in buying cheap and selling dear.

"The smaller sellers acquire habits of injurious idleness, waiting often for hours for customers. And this evil is experienced to a considerable extent even amongst the class of wholesale dealers.

"There are, also, by this arrangement, many more establishments for selling than are necessary in the villages, towns, and cities; and a very large capital is thus wasted without benefit to society. And from their number opposed to each other all over the country to obtain customers, they endeavor to undersell each other, and are therefore continually endeavoring to injure the producer by the establishment of what are called cheap shops and warehouses; and to support their character the master or his servants must be continually on the watch to buy bargains, that is, to procure wealth for less than the cost of its production.

"The distributers, small, medium, and large, have all to be supported by the producers, and the greater the number of the former compared with the latter, the greater will be the burden which the producer has to sustain; for as the number of distributers increases, the accumulation of wealth must decrease, and more must be required from the producer.

"The distributers of wealth, under the present system, are a dead weight upon the producers, and are most active demoralisers of society. Their dependent condition, at the commencement of their task, teaches or induces them to be servile to their customers, and to continue to be so as long as they are accumulating wealth by their cheap buying and dear selling. But when they have secured sufficient to be what they imagine to be an independence—to live without business—they are too often filled with a most ignorant pride, and become insolent to their dependents.

"The arrangement is altogether a most improvident one for society, whose interest it is to produce the greatest amount of wealth of the best qualities; while the existing system of distribution is not only to withdraw great numbers from producing to become distributers, but to add to the cost of the consumer all the expense of a most wasteful and extravagant distribution; the distribution costing to the consumer many times the price of the original cost of the wealth purchased.

"Then, by the position in which the seller is placed by his created desire for gain on the one hand, and the competition he meets with from opponents selling similar productions on the other, he is strongly tempted to deteriorate the articles which he has for sale; and when these are provisions, either of home production or of foreign importation, the effects upon the health, and consequent comfort and happiness of the consumers, are often most injurious, and productive of much premature death, especially among the working classes, who, in this respect, are perhaps made to be the greatest sufferers, by purchasing the inferior or low-priced articles.

"The expense of thus distributing wealth in Great Britain and Ireland, including transit from place to place, and all the agents directly and indirectly engaged in this department, is, perhaps, little short of one hundred millions annually, without taking into consideration the deterioration of the quality of many of the articles constituting this wealth, by carriage, and by being divided into small quantities, and kept in improper stores and places, in which the atmosphere is unfavorable to the keeping of such articles in a tolerably good, and much less in the best, condition for use."

In further illustration of the contrariety of interests between person and person, class and class, which pervades the present constitution of society, M. Considérant adds:—

"If the wine-growers wish for free trade, this freedom ruins the producer of corn, the manufacturers of iron, of cloth, of cotton, and—we are compelled to add—the smuggler and the customs' officer. If it is the interest of the consumer that machines should be invented which lower prices by rendering production less costly, these same machines throw out of work thousands of workmen who do not know how to, and cannot at once, find other work. Here, then, again is one of the innumerable vicious circles of civilisation ... for there are a thousand facts which prove cumulatively that in our existing social system the introduction of any good brings always along with it some evil.

"In short, if we go lower down and come to vulgar details, we find that it is the interest of the tailor, the shoemaker, and the hatter that coats, shoes, and hats should be soon worn out; that the glazier profits by the hail-storms which break windows; that the mason and the architect profit by fires; the lawyer is enriched by law-suits; the doctor by disease; the wine-seller by drunkenness; the prostitute by debauchery. And what a disaster it would be for the judges, the police, and the jailers, as well as for the barristers and the solicitors, and all the lawyers' clerks, if crimes, offences, and law-suits were all at once to come to an end!"

The following is one of the cardinal points of this school:—

"Add to all this, that civilisation, which sows dissension and war on every side; which employs a great part of its powers in unproductive labor or even in destruction; which furthermore diminishes the public wealth by the unnecessary friction and discord it introduces into industry; add to all this, I say, that this same social system has for its special characteristic to produce a repugnance for work—a disgust for labor.

"Everywhere you hear the laborer, the artisan, the clerk complain of his position and his occupation, while they long for the time when they can retire from work imposed upon them by necessity. To be repugnant, to have for its motive and pivot nothing but the fear of starvation, is the great, the fatal, characteristic of civilised labor. The civilised workman is condemned to penal servitude. So long as productive labor is so organized that instead of being associated with pleasure it is associated with pain, weariness and dislike, it will always happen that all will avoid it who are able. With few exceptions, those only will consent to work who are compelled to it by want. Hence the most numerous classes, the artificers of social wealth, the active and direct creators of all comfort and luxury, will always be condemned to touch closely on poverty and hunger; they will always be the slaves to ignorance and degradation; they will continue to be always that huge herd of mere beasts of burden whom we see ill-grown, decimated by disease, bowed down in the great workshop of society over the plow or over the counter, that they may prepare the delicate food, and the sumptuous enjoyments of the upper and idle classes.

"So long as no method of attractive labor has been devised, it will continue to be true that 'there must be many poor in order that there may be a few rich;' a mean and hateful saying, which we hear every day quoted as an eternal truth from the mouths of people who call themselves Christians or philosophers. It is very easy to understand that oppression, trickery, and especially poverty, are the permanent and fatal appanage of every state of society characterized by the dislike of work, for, in this case, there is nothing but poverty that will force men to labor. And the proof of this is, that if every one of all the workers were to become suddenly rich, nineteen-twentieths of all the work now done would be abandoned."

In the opinion of the Fourierists, the tendency of the present order of society is to a concentration of wealth in the hands of a comparatively few immensely rich individuals or companies, and the reduction of all the rest of the community into a complete dependence on them. This was termed by Fourier la jeodalite industrielle.

"This feudalism," says M. Considérant, "would be constituted as soon as the largest part of the industrial and territorial property of the nation belongs to a minority which absorbs all its revenues, while the great majority, chained to the work-bench or laboring on the soil, must be content to gnaw the pittance which is cast to them."

This disastrous result is to be brought about partly by the mere progress of competition, as sketched in our previous extract by M. Louis Blanc; assisted by the progress of national debts, which M. Considérant regards as mortgages of the whole land and capital of the country, of which "les capitalistes prêteurs" become, in a greater and greater measure, co-proprietors, receiving without labor or risk an increasing portion of the revenues.

THE SOCIALIST OBJECTIONS TO THE PRESENT ORDER OF SOCIETY EXAMINED

It is impossible to deny that the considerations brought to notice in the preceding chapter make out a frightful case either against the existing order of society, or against the position of man himself in this world. How much of the evils should be referred to the one, and how much to the other, is the principal theoretic question which has to be resolved. But the strongest case is susceptible of exaggeration; and it will have been evident to many readers, even from the passages I have quoted, that such exaggeration is not wanting in the representations of the ablest and most candid Socialists. Though much of their allegations is unanswerable, not a little is the result of errors in political economy; by which, let me say once for all, I do not mean the rejection of any practical rules of policy which have been laid down by political economists, I mean ignorance of economic facts, and of the causes by which the economic phenomena of society as it is, are actually determined.

In the first place it is unhappily true that the wages of ordinary labor, in all the countries of Europe, are wretchedly insufficient to supply the physical and moral necessities of the population in any tolerable measure. But, when it is further alleged that even this insufficient remuneration has a tendency to diminish; that there is, in the words of M. Louis Blanc, une baisse continue des salaires; the assertion is in opposition to all accurate information, and to many notorious facts. It has yet to be proved that there is any country in the civilized world where the ordinary wages of labor, estimated either in money or in articles of consumption, are declining; while in many they are, on the whole, on the increase; and an increase which is becoming, not slower, but more rapid. There are, occasionally, branches of industry which are being gradually superseded by something else, and, in those, until production accommodates itself to demand, wages are depressed; which is an evil, but a temporary one, and would admit of great alleviation even in the present system of social economy. A diminution thus produced of the reward of labor in some particular employment is the effect and the evidence of increased remuneration, or of a new source of remuneration, in some other; the total and the average remuneration being undiminished, or even increased. To make out an appearance of diminution in the rate of wages in any leading branch of industry, it is always found necessary to compare some month or year of special and temporary depression at the present time, with the average rate, or even some exceptionally high rate, at an earlier time. The vicissitudes are no doubt a great evil, but they were as frequent and as severe in former periods of economical history as now. The greater scale of the transactions, and the greater number of persons involved in each fluctuation, may make the fluctuation appear greater, but though a larger population affords more sufferers, the evil does not weigh heavier on each of them individually. There is much evidence of improvement, and none, that is at all trustworthy, of deterioration, in the mode of living of the laboring population of the countries of Europe; when there is any appearance to the contrary it is local or partial, and can always be traced either to the pressure of some temporary calamity, or to some bad law or unwise act of government which admits of being corrected, while the permanent causes all operate in the direction of improvement.

M. Louis Blanc, therefore, while showing himself much more enlightened than the older school of levellers and democrats, inasmuch as he recognizes the connection between low wages and the over-rapid increase of population, appears to have fallen into the same error which was at first committed by Malthus and his followers, that of supposing that because population has a greater power of increase than subsistence, its pressure upon subsistence must be always growing more severe. The difference is that the early Malthusians thought this an irrepressible tendency, while M. Louis Blanc thinks that it can be repressed, but only under a system of Communism. It is a great point gained for truth when it comes to be seen that the tendency to over-population is a fact which Communism, as well as the existing order of society, would have to deal with. And it is much to be rejoiced at that this necessity is admitted by the most considerable chiefs of all existing schools of Socialism. Owen and Fourier, no less than M. Louis Blanc, admitted it, and claimed for their respective systems a pre-eminent power of dealing with this difficulty. However this may be, experience shows that in the existing state of society the pressure of population on subsistence, which is the principal cause of low wages, though a great, is not an increasing evil; on the contrary, the progress of all that is called civilization has a tendency to diminish it, partly by the more rapid increase of the means of employing and maintaining labor, partly by the increased facilities opened to labor for transporting itself to new countries

44

and unoccupied fields of employment, and partly by a general improvement in the intelligence and prudence of the population. This progress, no doubt, is slow; but it is much that such progress should take place at all, while we are still only in the first stage of that public movement for the education of the whole people, which when more advanced must add greatly to the force of all the two causes of improvement specified above. It is, of course, open to discussion what form of society has the greatest power of dealing successfully with the pressure of population on subsistence, and on this question there is much to be said for Socialism; what was long thought to be its weakest point will, perhaps, prove to be one of its strongest. But it has no just claim to be considered as the sole means of preventing the general and growing degradation of the mass of mankind through the peculiar tendency of poverty to produce over-population. Society as at present constituted is not descending into that abyss, but gradually, though slowly, rising out of it, and this improvement is likely to be progressive if bad laws do not interfere with it.

Next, it must be observed that Socialists generally, and even the most enlightened of them, have a very imperfect and one-sided notion of the operation of competition. They see half its effects, and overlook the other half; they regard it as an agency for grinding down every one's remuneration—for obliging every one to accept less wages for his labor, or a less price for his commodities, which would be true only if every one had to dispose of his labor or his commodities to some great monopolist, and the competition were all on one side. They forget that competition is a cause of high prices and values as well as of low; that the buyers of labor

45

and of commodities compete with one another as well as the sellers; and that if it is competition which keeps the prices of labor and commodities as low as they are, it is competition which prevents them from falling still lower. In truth, when competition is perfectly free on both sides, its tendency is not specially either to raise or to lower the price of articles, but to equalize it; to level inequalities of remuneration, and to reduce all to a general average, a result which, in so far as realized (no doubt very imperfectly), is, on Socialistic principles, desirable. But if, disregarding for the time that part of the effects of competition which consists in keeping up prices, we fix our attention on its effect in keeping them down, and contemplate this effect in reference solely to the interest of the laboring classes, it would seem that if competition keeps down wages, and so gives a motive to the laboring classes to withdraw the labor market from the full influence of competition, if they can, it must on the other hand have credit for keeping down the prices of the articles on which wages are expended, to the great advantage of those who depend on wages. To meet this consideration Socialists, as we said in our quotation from M. Louis Blanc, are reduced to affirm that the low prices of commodities produced by competition are delusive and lead in the end to higher prices than before, because when the richest competitor has got rid of all his rivals, he commands the market and can demand any price he pleases. Now, the commonest experience shows that this state of things, under really free competition, is wholly imaginary. The richest competitor neither does nor can get rid of all his rivals, and establish himself in exclusive possession of the market; and it is not the fact that any important branch of industry or commerce formerly divided among many has become, or shows any tendency to become, the monopoly of a few.

The kind of policy described is sometimes possible where, as in the case of railways, the only competition possible is between two or three great companies, the operations being on too vast a scale to be within the reach of individual capitalists; and this is one of the reasons why businesses which require to be carried on by great joint-stock enterprises cannot be trusted to competition, but, when not reserved by the State to itself, ought to be carried on under conditions prescribed, and, from time to time, varied by the State, for the purpose of insuring to the public a cheaper supply of its wants than would be afforded by private interest in the absence of sufficient competition. But in the ordinary branches of industry no one rich competitor has it in his power to drive out all the smaller ones. Some businesses show a tendency to pass out of the hands of many small producers or dealers into a smaller number of larger ones; but the cases in which this happens are those in which the possession of a larger capital permits the adoption of more powerful machinery, more efficient by more expensive processes, or a better organized and more economical mode of carrying on business, and thus enables the large dealer legitimately and permanently to supply the commodity cheaper than can be done on the small scale; to the great advantage of the consumers, and therefore of the laboring classes, and diminishing, pro tanto, that waste of the resources of the community so much complained of by Socialists, the unnecessary multiplication of mere distributors, and of the various other classes whom Fourier calls the parasites of industry. When this change is effected, the larger capitalists, either individual or joint stock, among which the business is divided, are seldom, if ever, in any considerable branch of commerce, so few as that competition shall not continue to act between them; so that the saving in cost, which enabled them to undersell the small dealers, continues afterwards, as at first, to be passed on, in lower prices, to their customers. The operation, therefore, of competition in keeping down the prices of commodities, including those on which wages are expended, is not illusive but real, and, we may add, is a growing, not a declining, fact.

But there are other respects, equally important, in which the charges brought by Socialists against competition do not admit of so complete an answer. Competition is the best security for cheapness, but by no means a security for quality. In former times, when producers and consumers were less numerous, it was a security for both. The market was not large enough nor the means of publicity sufficient to enable a dealer to make a fortune by continually attracting new customers: his success depended on his retaining those that he had; and when a dealer furnished good articles, or when he did not, the fact was soon known to those whom it concerned, and he acquired a character for honest or dishonest dealing of more importance to him than the gain that would be made by cheating casual purchasers. But on the great scale of modern transactions, with the great multiplication of competition and the immense increase in the quantity of business competed for, dealers are so little dependent on permanent customers that character is much less essential to them, while there is also far less certainty of their obtaining the character they deserve. The low prices which a tradesman advertises are known, to a thousand for one who has discovered for himself or learned from others, that the bad quality of the goods is more than an equivalent for their cheapness; while at the same time the much greater fortunes now made by some dealers excite the cupidity of all, and the greed of rapid gain substitutes itself for the modest desire to make a living by their business. In this manner, as wealth increases and greater prizes seem to be within reach, more and more of a gambling spirit is introduced into commerce; and where this prevails not only are the simplest maxims of prudence disregarded, but all, even the most perilous, forms of pecuniary improbity receive a terrible stimulus. This is the meaning of what is called the intensity of modern competition. It is further to be mentioned that when this intensity has reached a certain height, and when a portion of the producers of an article or the dealers in it have resorted to any of the modes of fraud, such as adulteration, giving short measure, &c., of the increase of which there is now so much complaint, the temptation is immense on these to adopt the fraudulent practises, who would not have originated them; for the public are aware of the low prices fallaciously produced by the frauds, but do not find out at first, if ever, that the article is not worth the lower price, and they will not go on paying a higher price for a better article, and the honest dealer is placed at a terrible disadvantage. Thus the frauds, begun by a few, become customs of the trade, and the morality of the trading classes is more and more deteriorated.

On this point, therefore, Socialists have really made out the existence not only of a great evil, but of one which grows and tends to grow with the growth of population and wealth. It must be said, however, that society has never yet used the means which are already in its power of grappling with this evil. The laws against commercial

49

frauds are very defective, and their execution still more so. Laws of this description have no chance of being really enforced unless it is the special duty of some one to enforce them. They are specially in need of a public prosecutor. It is still to be discovered how far it is possible to repress by means of the criminal law a class of misdeeds which are now seldom brought before the tribunals, and to which, when brought, the judicial administration of this country is most unduly lenient. The most important class, however, of these frauds, to the mass of the people, those which affect the price or quality of articles of daily consumption, can be in a great measure overcome by the institution of co-operative stores. By this plan any body of consumers who form themselves into an association for the purpose, are enabled to pass over the retail dealers and obtain their articles direct from the wholesale merchants, or, what is better (now that wholesale co-operative agencies have been established), from the producers, thus freeing themselves from the heavy tax now paid to the distributing classes and at the same time eliminate the usual perpetrators of adulterations and other frauds. Distribution thus becomes a work performed by agents selected and paid by those who have no interest in anything but the cheapness and goodness of the article; and the distributors are capable of being thus reduced to the numbers which the quantity of work to be done really requires. The difficulties of the plan consist in the skill and trustworthiness required in the managers, and the imperfect nature of the control which can be exercised over them by the body at large. The great success and rapid growth of the system prove, however, that these difficulties are, in some tolerable degree, overcome. At all events, if the beneficial tendency of the competition of retailers in promoting cheapness is fore-gone, and has to be replaced by other securities, the mischievous tendency of the same competition in deteriorating quality is at any rate got rid of; and the prosperity of the co-operative stores shows that this benefit is obtained not only without detriment to cheapness, but with great advantage to it, since the profits of the concerns enable them to return to the consumers a large percentage on the price of every article supplied to them. So far, therefore, as this class of evils is concerned, an effectual remedy is already in operation, which, though suggested by and partly grounded on socialistic principles, is consistent with the existing constitution of property.

With regard to those greater and more conspicuous economical frauds, or malpractices equivalent to frauds, of which so many deplorable cases have become notorious—committed by merchants and bankers between themselves or between them and those who have trusted them with money, such a remedy as above described is not available, and the only resources which the present constitution of society affords against them are a sterner reprobation by opinion, and a more efficient repression by the law. Neither of these remedies has had any approach to an effectual trial. It is on the occurrence of insolvencies that these dishonest practices usually come to light; the perpetrators take their place, not in the class of malefactors, but in that of insolvent debtors; and the laws of this and other countries were formerly so savage against simple insolvency, that by one of those reactions to which the opinions of mankind are liable, insolvents came to be regarded mainly as objects of compassion, and it seemed to be thought that the hand both of law and of public opinion could hardly press too lightly upon

51

them. By an error in a contrary direction to the ordinary one of our law, which in the punishment of offences in general wholly neglects the question of reparation to the sufferer, our bankruptcy laws have for some time treated the recovery for creditors of what is left of their property as almost the sole object, scarcely any importance being attached to the punishment of the bankrupt for any misconduct which does not directly interfere with that primary purpose. For three or four years past there has been a slight counter-reaction, and more than one bankruptcy act has been passed, somewhat less indulgent to the bankrupt; but the primary object regarded has still been the pecuniary interest of the creditors, and criminality in the bankrupt himself, with the exception of a small number of well-marked offences, gets off almost with impunity. It may be confidently affirmed, therefore, that, at least in this country, society has not exerted the power it possesses of making mercantile dishonesty dangerous to the perpetrator. On the contrary, it is a gambling trick in which all the advantage is on the side of the trickster: if the trick succeeds it makes his fortune, or preserves it; if it fails, he is at most reduced to poverty, which was perhaps already impending when he determined to run the chance, and he is classed by those who have not looked closely into the matter, and even by many who have, not among the infamous but among the unfortunate. Until a more moral and rational mode of dealing with culpable insolvency has been tried and failed, commercial dishonesty cannot be ranked among evils the prevalence of which is inseparable from commercial competition.

Another point on which there is much misapprehension on the part of Socialists, as well as of Trades Unionists and other partisans of Labor against Capital, relates to the proportions in which the produce of the country is really shared and the amount of what is actually diverted from those who produce it, to enrich other persons. I forbear for the present to speak of the land, which is a subject apart. But with respect to capital employed in business, there is in the popular notions a great deal of illusion. When, for instance, a capitalist invests £20,000 in his business, and draws from it an income of (suppose) £2,000 a year, the common impression is as if he was the beneficial owner both of the £20,000 and of the £2,000, while the laborers own nothing but their wages. The truth, however, is, that he only obtains the £2,000 on condition of applying no part of the £20,000 to his own use. He has the legal control over it, and might squander it if he chose, but if he did he would not have the £2,000 a year also. As long as he derives an income from his capital he has not the option of withholding it from the use of others. As much of his invested capital as consists of buildings, machinery, and other instruments of production, are applied to production and are not applicable to the support or enjoyment of any one. What is so applicable (including what is laid out in keeping up or renewing the buildings and instruments) is paid away to laborers, forming their remuneration and their share in the division of the produce. For all personal purposes they have the capital and he has but the profits, which it only yields to him on condition that the capital itself is employed in satisfying not his own wants, but those of laborers. The proportion which the profits of capital usually bear to capital itself (or rather to the circulating portion of it) is the ratio which the capitalist's share of the produce bears to the aggregate share of the laborers. Even of his own share a small part only belongs to him as the owner of capital. The portion of the produce

53

which falls to capital merely as capital is measured by the interest of money, since that is all that the owner of capital obtains when he contributes nothing to production except the capital itself. Now the interest of capital in the public funds, which are considered to be the best security, is at the present prices (which have not varied much for many years) about three and one-third per cent. Even in this investment there is some little risk—risk of repudiation, risk of being obliged to sell out at a low price in some commercial crisis.

Estimating these risks at 1/3 per cent., the remaining 3 per cent. may be considered as the remuneration of capital, apart from insurance against loss. On the security of a mortgage 4 per cent. is generally obtained, but in this transaction there are considerably greater risks—the uncertainty of titles to land under our bad system of law; the chance of having to realize the security at a great cost in law charges; and liability to delay in the receipt of the interest even when the principal is safe. When mere money independently of exertion yields a larger income, as it sometimes does, for example, by shares in railway or other companies, the surplus is hardly ever an equivalent for the risk of losing the whole, or part, of the capital by mismanagement, as in the case of the Brighton Railway, the dividend of which, after having been 6 per cent. per annum, sunk to from nothing to 1-1/2 per cent., and shares which had been bought at 120 could not be sold for more than about 43. When money is lent at the high rates of interest one occasionally hears of, rates only given by spend-thrifts and needy persons, it is because the risk of loss is so great that few who possess money can be induced to lend to them at all. So little reason is there for the outcry against "usury" as one of the grievous burthens of the working-classes. Of the profits, therefore, which a manufacturer or other person in business obtains from his capital no more than about 3 per cent. can be set down to the capital itself. If he were able and willing to give up the whole of this to his laborers, who already share among them the whole of his capital as it is annually reproduced from year to year, the addition to their weekly wages would be inconsiderable. Of what he obtains beyond 3 per cent. a great part is insurance against the manifold losses he is exposed to, and cannot safely be applied to his own use, but requires to be kept in reserve to cover those losses when they occur. The remainder is properly the remuneration of his skill and industry—the wages of his labor of superintendence. No doubt if he is very successful in business these wages of his are extremely liberal, and quite out of proportion to what the same skill and industry would command if offered for hire. But, on the other hand, he runs a worse risk than that of being out of employment; that of doing the work without earning anything by it, of having the labor and anxiety without the wages. I do not say that the drawbacks balance the privileges, or that he derives no advantage from the position which makes him a capitalist and employer of labor, instead of a skilled superintendent letting out his services to others; but the amount of his advantage must not be estimated by the great prizes alone. If we subtract from the gains of some the losses of others, and deduct from the balance a fair compensation for the anxiety, skill, and labor of both, grounded on the market price of skilled superintendence, what remains will be, no doubt, considerable, but yet, when compared to the entire capital of the country, annually reproduced and dispensed in wages, it is very much smaller than it

55

appears to the popular imagination; and were the whole of it added to the share of the laborers it would make a less addition to that share than would be made by any important invention in machinery, or by the suppression of unnecessary distributors and other "parasites of industry." To complete the estimate, however, of the portion of the produce of industry which goes to remunerate capital we must not stop at the interest earned out of the produce by the capital actually employed in producing it, but must include that which is paid to the former owners of capital which has been unproductively spent and no longer exists, and is paid, of course, out of the produce of other capital. Of this nature is the interest of national debts, which is the cost a nation is burthened with for past difficulties and dangers, or for past folly or profligacy of its rulers, more or less shared by the nation itself. To this must be added the interest on the debts of landowners and other unproductive consumers; except so far as the money borrowed may have been spent in remunerative improvement of the productive powers of the land. As for landed property itself—the appropriation of the rent of land by private individuals—I reserve, as I have said, this question for discussion hereafter; for the tenure of land might be varied in any manner considered desirable, all the land might be declared the property of the State, without interfering with the right of property in anything which is the product of human labor and abstinence.

It seemed desirable to begin the discussion of the Socialist question by these remarks in abatement of Socialist exaggerations, in order that the true issues between Socialism and the existing state of society might be correctly conceived. The present system is not, as many Socialists believe, hurrying us into a state of general indigence and slavery from which only Socialism can save us. The evils and injustices suffered under the present system are great, but they are not increasing; on the contrary, the general tendency is towards their slow diminution. Moreover the inequalities in the distribution of the produce between capital and labor, however they may shock the feeling of natural justice, would not by their mere equalisation afford by any means so large a fund for raising the lower levels of remuneration as Socialists, and many besides Socialists, are apt to suppose. There is not any one abuse or injustice now prevailing in society by merely abolishing which the human race would pass out of suffering into happiness. What is incumbent on us is a calm comparison between two different systems of society, with a view of determining which of them affords the greatest resources for overcoming the inevitable difficulties of life. And if we find the answer to this question more difficult, and more dependent upon intellectual and moral conditions, than is usually thought, it is satisfactory to reflect that there is time before us for the question to work itself out on an experimental scale, by actual trial. I believe we shall find that no other test is possible of the practicability or beneficial operation of Socialist arrangements; but that the intellectual and moral grounds of Socialism deserve the most attentive study, as affording in many cases the guiding principles of the improvements necessary to give the present economic system of society its best chance.

THE DIFFICULTIES OF SOCIALISM

Among those who call themselves Socialists, two kinds of persons may be distinguished. There are, in the first place, those whose plans for a new order of society, in which private property and individual competition are to be superseded and other motives to action substituted, are on the scale of a village community or township, and would be applied to an entire country by the multiplication of such self-acting units; of this character are the systems of Owen, of Fourier, and the more thoughtful and philosophic Socialists generally. The other class, who are more a product of the Continent than of Great Britain and may be called the revolutionary Socialists, propose to themselves a much bolder stroke. Their scheme is the management of the whole productive resources of the country by one central authority, the general government. And with this view some of them avow as their purpose that the working classes, or somebody in their behalf, should take possession of all the property of the country, and administer it for the general benefit.

Whatever be the difficulties of the first of these two forms of Socialism, the second must evidently involve the same difficulties and many more. The former, too, has the great advantage that it can be brought into operation progressively, and can prove its capabilities by trial. It can be tried first on a select population and extended to others as their education and cultivation permit. It need not, and in the natural order of things would not, become an engine of subversion until it had shown itself capable of being also a means of reconstruction. It is not so with the other: the aim of that is to substitute the new rule for the old at a single stroke, and to exchange the amount of good realised under the present system, and its large possibilities of improvement, for a plunge without any preparation into the most extreme form of the problem of carrying on the whole round of the operations of social life without the motive power which has always hitherto worked the social machinery. It must be acknowledged that those who would play this game on the strength of their own private opinion, unconfirmed as yet by any experimental verification—who would forcibly deprive all who have now a comfortable physical existence of their only present means of preserving it, and would brave the frightful bloodshed and misery that would ensue if the attempt was resisted—must have a serene confidence in their own wisdom on the one hand and a recklessness of other people's sufferings on the other, which Robespierre and St. Just, hitherto the typical instances of those united attributes, scarcely came up to. Nevertheless this scheme has great elements of popularity which the more cautious and reasonable form of Socialism has not; because what it professes to do it promises to do quickly, and holds out hope to the enthusiastic of seeing the whole of their aspirations realised in their own time and at a blow.

The peculiarities, however, of the revolutionary form of Socialism will be most conveniently examined after the considerations common to both the forms have been duly weighed.

The produce of the world could not attain anything approaching to its present amount, nor support anything approaching to the present number of its inhabitants, except upon two conditions: abundant and costly machinery, buildings, and other instruments of production; and the power of undertaking long operations and waiting a considerable time for their fruits. In other words, there must be a large accumulation of capital, both fixed in the implements and buildings, and circulating, that is employed in maintaining the laborers and their families during the time which elapses before the productive operations are completed and the products come in. This necessity depends on physical laws, and is inherent in the condition of human life; but these requisites of production, the capital, fixed and circulating, of the country (to which has to be added the land, and all that is contained in it), may either be the collective property of those who use it, or may belong to individuals; and the question is, which of these arrangements is most conducive to human happiness. What is characteristic of Socialism is the joint ownership by all the members of the community of the instruments and means of production; which carries with it the consequence that the division of the produce among the body of owners must be a public act, performed according to rules laid down by the community. Socialism by no means excludes private ownership of articles of consumption; the exclusive right of each to his or her share of the produce when received, either to enjoy, to give, or to exchange it. The land, for example, might be wholly the property of the community for agricultural and other productive purposes, and might be cultivated on their joint account, and yet the dwelling assigned to each individual or family as part of their remuneration might be as exclusively theirs, while they continued to fulfil their share of the common labors, as any one's house now is; and not the dwelling only, but any ornamental ground which the circumstances of the association allowed to be attached to the house for purposes of enjoyment. The distinctive feature of Socialism is not that all things are in common, but that production is only carried on upon the common account, and that the instruments of production are held as common property. The practicability then of Socialism, on the scale of Mr. Owen's or M. Fourier's villages, admits of no dispute. The attempt to manage the whole production of a nation by one central organization is a totally different matter; but a mixed agricultural and manufacturing association of from two thousand to four thousand inhabitants under any tolerable circumstances of soil and climate would be easier to manage than many a joint stock company. The question to be considered is, whether this joint management is likely to be as efficient and successful as the managements of private industry by private capital. And this question has to be considered in a double aspect; the efficiency of the directing mind, or minds, and that of the simple workpeople. And in order to state this question in its simplest form, we will suppose the form of Socialism to be simple Communism, i.e. equal division of the produce among all the sharers, or, according to M. Louis Blanc's still higher standard of justice, apportionment of it according to difference of need, but without making any difference of reward according to the nature of the duty nor according to the supposed merits or services of the individual. There are other forms of Socialism, particularly Fourierism, which do, on considerations of justice or expediency, allow differences of remuneration for different kinds or degrees of service to the community; but the consideration of these may be for the present postponed.

The difference between the motive powers in the

economy of society under private property and under Communism would be greatest in the case of the directing minds. Under the present system, the direction being entirely in the hands of the person or persons who own (or are personally responsible for) the capital, the whole benefit of the difference between the best administration and the worst under which the business can continue to be carried on accrues to the person or persons who control the administration: they reap the whole profit of good management except so far as their self-interest or liberality induce them to share it with their subordinates; and they suffer the whole detriment of mismanagement except so far as this may cripple their subsequent power of employing labor. This strong personal motive to do their very best and utmost for the efficiency and economy of the operations, would not exist under Communism; as the managers would only receive out of the produce the same equal dividend as the other members of the association. What would remain would be the interest common to all in so managing affairs as to make the dividend as large as possible; the incentives of public spirit, of conscience, and of the honor and credit of the managers. The force of these motives, especially when combined, is great. But it varies greatly in different persons, and is much greater for some purposes than for others. The verdict of experience, in the imperfect degree of moral cultivation which mankind have yet reached, is that the motive of conscience and that of credit and reputation, even when they are of some strength, are, in the majority of cases, much stronger as restraining than as impelling forces—are more to be depended on for preventing wrong, than for calling forth the fullest energies in the pursuit of ordinary occupations. In the case of most men the only inducement which has been found sufficiently constant and unflagging to overcome the ever-present influence of indolence and love of ease, and induce men to apply themselves unrelaxingly to work for the most part in itself dull and unexciting, is the prospect of bettering their own economic condition and that of their family; and the closer the connection of every increase of exertion with a corresponding increase of its fruits, the more powerful is this motive. To suppose the contrary would be to imply that with men as they now are, duty and honor are more powerful principles of action than personal interest, not solely as to special acts and forbearances respecting which those sentiments have been exceptionally cultivated, but in the regulation of their whole lives; which no one, I suppose, will affirm. It may be said that this inferior efficacy of public and social feelings is not inevitable—is the result of imperfect education. This I am quite ready to admit, and also that there are even now many individual exceptions to the general infirmity. But before these exceptions can grow into a majority, or even into a very large minority, much time will be required. The education of human beings is one of the most difficult of all arts, and this is one of the points in which it has hitherto been least successful; moreover improvements in general education are necessarily very gradual because the future generation is educated by the present, and the imperfections of the teachers set an invincible limit to the degree in which they can train their pupils to be better than themselves. We must therefore expect, unless we are operating upon a select portion of the population, that personal interest will for a long time be a more effective stimulus to the most vigorous and careful conduct of the industrial business of society than motives of a higher character. It will be said that at present the greed of personal gain by its very excess counteracts its own end by the stimulus it gives to reckless and often dishonest risks. This it does, and under Communism that source of evil would generally be absent. It is probable, indeed, that enterprise either of a bad or of a good kind would be a deficient element, and that business in general would fall very much under the dominion of routine; the rather, as the performance of duty in such communities has to be enforced by external sanctions, the more nearly each person's duty can be reduced to fixed rules, the easier it is to hold him to its performance. A circumstance which increases the probability of this result is the limited power which the managers would have of independent action. They would of course hold their authority from the choice of the community, by whom their function might at any time be withdrawn from them; and this would make it necessary for them, even if not so required by the constitution of the community, to obtain the general consent of the body before making any change in the established mode of carrying on the concern. The difficulty of persuading a numerous body to make a change in their accustomed mode of working, of which change the trouble is often great, and the risk more obvious to their minds than the advantage, would have a great tendency to keep things in their accustomed track. Against this it has to be set, that choice by the persons who are directly interested in the success of the work, and who have practical knowledge and opportunities of judgment, might be expected on the average to produce managers of greater skill than the chances of birth, which now so often determine who shall be the owner of the capital. This may be true; and though it may be replied that the capitalist by inheritance can also, like the community, appoint a manager more capable than himself, this would only place him on the same level of advantage as the community, not on a higher level. But it must be said on the other side that under the Communist system the persons most qualified for the management would be likely very often to hang back from undertaking it. At present the manager, even if he be a hired servant, has a very much larger remuneration than the other persons concerned in the business; and there are open to his ambition higher social positions to which his function of manager is a stepping-stone. On the Communist system none of these advantages would be possessed by him; he could obtain only the same dividend out of the produce of the community's labor as any other member of it; he would no longer have the chance of raising himself from a receiver of wages into the class of capitalists; and while he could be in no way better off than any other laborer, his responsibilities and anxieties would be so much greater that a large proportion of mankind would be likely to prefer the less onerous position. This difficulty was foreseen by Plato as an objection to the system proposed in his Republic of community of goods among a governing class; and the motive on which he relied for inducing the fit persons to take on themselves, in the absence of all the ordinary inducements, the cares and labors of government, was the fear of being governed by worse men. This, in truth, is the motive which would have to be in the main depended upon; the persons most competent to the management would be prompted to undertake the office to prevent it from falling into less competent hands. And the motive would probably be effectual at times when there was an impression that by incompetent management the affairs of the community were going to ruin, or even only decidedly deteriorating. But this motive could not, as a rule, expect to be called into action by the less stringent inducement of merely promoting improvement; unless in the case of inventors or schemers eager to try some device from which they hoped for great and immediate fruits; and persons of this kind are very often unfitted by over-sanguine temper and imperfect judgment for the general conduct of affairs, while even when fitted for it they are precisely the kind of persons against whom the average man is apt to entertain a prejudice, and they would often be unable to overcome the preliminary difficulty of persuading the community both to adopt their project and to accept them as managers. Communistic management would thus be, in all probability, less favorable than private management to that striking out of new paths and making immediate sacrifices for distant and uncertain advantages, which, though seldom unattended with risk, is generally indispensable to great improvements in the economic condition of mankind, and even to keeping up the existing state in the face of a continual increase of the number of mouths to be fed.

We have thus far taken account only of the operation of motives upon the managing minds of the association. Let us now consider how the case stands in regard to the ordinary workers.

These, under Communism, would have no interest, except their share of the general interest, in doing their work honestly and energetically. But in this respect matters would be no worse than they now are in regard to the great majority of the producing classes. These, being paid by fixed wages, are so far from having any direct interest of their own in the efficiency of their work, that they have not even that share in the general interest

66

which every worker would have in the Communistic organization. Accordingly, the inefficiency of hired labor, the imperfect manner in which it calls forth the real capabilities of the laborers, is matter of common remark. It is true that a character for being a good workman is far from being without its value, as it tends to give him a preference in employment, and sometimes obtains for him higher wages. There are also possibilities of rising to the position of foreman, or other subordinate administrative posts, which are not only more highly paid than ordinary labor, but sometimes open the way to ulterior advantages. But on the other side is to be set that under Communism the general sentiment of the community, composed of the comrades under whose eyes each person works, would be sure to be in favor of good and hard working, and unfavorable to laziness, carelessness, and waste. In the present system not only is this not the case, but the public opinion of the workman class often acts in the very opposite direction: the rules of some trade societies actually forbid their members to exceed a certain standard of efficiency, lest they should diminish the number of laborers required for the work; and for the same reason they often violently resist contrivances for economising labor. The change from this to a state in which every person would have an interest in rendering every other person as industrious, skilful, and careful as possible (which would be the case under Communism), would be a change very much for the better.

It is, however, to be considered that the principal defects of the present system in respect to the efficiency of labor may be corrected, and the chief advantages of Communism in that respect may be obtained, by arrangements compatible with private property and individual competition. Considerable improvement is already obtained by piece-work, in the kinds of labor which admit of it. By this the workman's personal interest is closely connected with the quantity of work he turns out—not so much with its quality, the security for which still has to depend on the employer's vigilance; neither does piece-work carry with it the public opinion of the workman class, which is often, on the contrary, strongly opposed to it, as a means of (as they think) diminishing the market for laborers. And there is really good ground for their dislike of piece-work, if, as is alleged, it is a frequent practice of employers, after using piece-work to ascertain the utmost which a good workman can do, to fix the price of piece-work so low that by doing that utmost he is not able to earn more than they would be obliged to give him as day wages for ordinary work.

But there is a far more complete remedy than piece-work for the disadvantages of hired labor, viz., what is now called industrial partnership—the admission of the whole body of laborers to a participation in the profits, by distributing among all who share in the work, in the form of a percentage on their earnings, the whole or a fixed portion of the gains after a certain remuneration has been allowed to the capitalist. This plan has been found of admirable efficacy, both in this country and abroad. It has enlisted the sentiments of the workmen employed on the side of the most careful regard by all of them to the general interest of the concern; and by its joint effect in promoting zealous exertion and checking waste, it has very materially increased the remuneration of every description of labor in the concerns in which it has been adopted. It is evident that this system admits of indefinite extension and of an indefinite increase in the share of profits assigned to the laborers, short of that which would leave to the managers less than the needful degree of personal interest in the success of the concern. It is even likely that when such arrangements become common, many of these concerns would at some period or another, on the death or retirement of the chief's pass, by arrangement, into the state of purely co-operative associations.

It thus appears that as far as concerns the motives to exertion in the general body, Communism has no advantage which may not be reached under private property, while as respects the managing heads it is at a considerable disadvantage. It has also some disadvantages which seem to be inherent in it, through the necessity under which it lies of deciding in a more or less arbitrary manner questions which, on the present system, decide themselves, often badly enough but spontaneously.

It is a simple rule, and under certain aspects a just one, to give equal payment to all who share in the work. But this is a very imperfect justice unless the work also is apportioned equally. Now the many different kinds of work required in every society are very unequal in hardness and unpleasantness. To measure these against one another, so as to make quality equivalent to quantity, is so difficult that Communists generally propose that all should work by turns at every kind of labor. But this involves an almost complete sacrifice of the economic advantages of the division of employments, advantages which are indeed frequently over-estimated (or rather the counter considerations are under-estimated) by political economists, but which are nevertheless, in the point of view of the productiveness of labor, very considerable, for the double reason that the co-operation of employment enables the work to distribute itself with some regard to

69

the special capacities and qualifications of the worker, and also that every worker acquires greater skill and rapidity in one kind of work by confining himself to it. The arrangement, therefore, which is deemed indispensable to a just distribution would probably be a very considerable disadvantage in respect of production. But further, it is still a very imperfect standard of justice to demand the same amount of work from every one. People have unequal capacities of work, both mental and bodily, and what is a light task for one is an insupportable burthen to another. It is necessary, therefore, that there should be a dispensing power, an authority competent to grant exemptions from the ordinary amount of work, and to proportion tasks in some measure to capabilities. As long as there are any lazy or selfish persons who like better to be worked for by others than to work, there will be frequent attempts to obtain exemptions by favor or fraud, and the frustration of these attempts will be an affair of considerable difficulty, and will by no means be always successful. These inconveniences would be little felt, for some time at least, in communities composed of select persons, earnestly desirous of the success of the experiment; but plans for the regeneration of society must consider average human beings, and not only them but the large residuum of persons greatly below the average in the personal and social virtues. The squabbles and ill-blood which could not fail to be engendered by the distribution of work whenever such persons have to be dealt with, would be a great abatement from the harmony and unanimity which Communists hope would be found among the members of their association. That concord would, even in the most fortunate circumstances, be much more liable to disturbance than Communists suppose.

The institution provides that there shall be no quarrelling about material interests; individualism is excluded from that department of affairs. But there are other departments from which no institutions can exclude it: there will still be rivalry for reputation and for personal power. When selfish ambition is excluded from the field in which, with most men, it chiefly exercises itself, that of riches and pecuniary interest, it would betake itself with greater intensity to the domain still open to it, and we may expect that the struggles for pre-eminence and for influence in the management would be of great bitterness when the personal passions, diverted from their ordinary channel, are driven to seek their principal gratification in that other direction. For these various reasons it is probable that a Communist association would frequently fail to exhibit the attractive picture of mutual love and unity of will and feeling which we are often told by Communists to expect, but would often be torn by dissension and not unfrequently broken up by it.

Other and numerous sources of discord are inherent in the necessity which the Communist principle involves, of deciding by the general voice questions of the utmost importance to every one, which on the present system can be and are left to individuals to decide, each for his own case. As an example, take the subject of education. All Socialists are strongly impressed with the all-importance of the training given to the young, not only for the reasons which apply universally, but because their demands being much greater than those of any other system upon the intelligence and morality of the individual citizen, they have even more at stake than any other societies on the excellence of their educational arrangements. Now under Communism these arrangements would have to be made

71

for every citizen by the collective body, since individual parents, supposing them to prefer some other mode of educating their children, would have no private means of paying for it, and would be limited to what they could do by their own personal teaching and influence. But every adult member of the body would have an equal voice in determining the collective system designed for the benefit of all. Here, then, is a most fruitful source of discord in every association. All who had any opinion or preference as to the education they would desire for their own children, would have to rely for their chance of obtaining it upon the influence they could exercise in the joint decision of the community.

It is needless to specify a number of other important questions affecting the mode of employing the productive resources of the association, the conditions of social life, the relations of the body with other associations, &c., on which difference of opinion, often irreconcilable, would be likely to arise. But even the dissensions which might be expected would be a far less evil to the prospects of humanity than a delusive unanimity produced by the prostration of all individual opinions and wishes before the decree of the majority. The obstacles to human progression are always great, and require a concurrence of favorable circumstances to overcome them; but an indispensable condition of their being overcome is, that human nature should have freedom to expand spontaneously in various directions, both in thought and practice; that people should both think for themselves and try experiments for themselves, and should not resign into the hands of rulers, whether acting in the name of a few or of the majority, the business of thinking for them, and of prescribing how they shall act. But in Communist associations private life would be brought in a most unexampled degree within the dominion of public authority, and there would be less scope for the development of individual character and individual preferences than has hitherto existed among the full citizens of any state belonging to the progressive branches of the human family. Already in all societies the compression of individuality by the majority is a great and growing evil; it would probably be much greater under Communism, except so far as it might be in the power of individuals to set bounds to it by selecting to belong to a community of persons like-minded with themselves.

From these various considerations I do not seek to draw any inference against the possibility that Communistic production is capable of being at some future time the form of society best adapted to the wants and circumstances of mankind. I think that this is, and will long be an open question, upon which fresh light will continually be obtained, both by trial of the Communistic principle under favorable circumstances, and by the improvements which will be gradually effected in the working of the existing system, that of private ownership. The one certainty is, that Communism, to be successful, requires a high standard of both moral and intellectual education in all the members of the community—moral, to qualify them for doing their part honestly and energetically in the labor of life under no inducement but their share in the general interest of the association, and their feelings of duty and sympathy towards it; intellectual, to make them capable of estimating distant interests and entering into complex considerations, sufficiently at least to be able to discriminate, in these matters, good counsel from bad. Now I reject altogether the notion that it is impossible for education and cultivation such as is implied in these things to be made the inheritance of every person in the nation; but I am convinced that it is very difficult, and that the passage to it from our present condition can only be slow. I admit the plea that in the points of moral education on which the success of communism depends, the present state of society is demoralizing, and that only a Communistic association can effectually train mankind for Communism. It is for Communism, then, to prove, by practical experiment, its power of giving this training. Experiments alone can show whether there is as yet in any portion of the population a sufficiently high level of moral cultivation to make Communism succeed, and to give to the next generation among themselves the education necessary to keep that high level permanently If Communist associations show that they can be durable and prosperous, they will multiply, and will probably be adopted by successive portions of the population of the more advanced countries as they become morally fitted for that mode of life. But to force unprepared populations into Communist societies, even if a political revolution gave the power to make such an attempt, would end in disappointment.

If practical trial is necessary to test the capabilities of Communism, it is no less required for those other forms of Socialism which recognize the difficulties of Communism and contrive means to surmount them. The principal of these is Fourierism, a system which, if only as a specimen of intellectual ingenuity, is highly worthy of the attention of any student, either of society or of the human mind. There is scarcely an objection or a difficulty which Fourier did not forsee, and against which he did not make provision beforehand by self-acting contrivances, grounded, however, upon a less high principle of distributive justice than that of Communism, since he admits inequalities of distribution and individual ownership of capital, but not the arbitrary disposal of it. The great problem which he grapples with is how to make labor attractive, since, if this could be done, the principal difficulty of Socialism would be overcome. He maintains that no kind of useful labor is necessarily or universally repugnant, unless either excessive in amount or devoid of the stimulus of companionship and emulation, or regarded by mankind with contempt. The workers in a Fourierist village are to class themselves spontaneously in groups, each group undertaking a different kind of work, and the same person may be a member not only of one group but of any number; a certain minimum having first been set apart for the subsistence of every member of the community, whether capable or not of labor, the society divides the remainder of the produce among the different groups, in such shares as it finds attract to each the amount of labor required, and no more; if there is too great a run upon particular groups it is a sign that those groups are over-remunerated relatively to others; if any are neglected their remuneration must be made higher. The share of produce assigned to each group is divided in fixed proportions among three elements—labor, capital, and talent; the part assigned to talent being awarded by the suffrages of the group itself, and it is hoped that among the variety of human capacities all, or nearly all, will be qualified to excel in some group or other. The remuneration for capital is to be such as is found sufficient to induce savings from individual consumption, in order to increase the common stock to such point as is desired. The number and ingenuity of the contrivances for meeting minor difficulties, and getting rid of minor inconveniencies, is very remarkable. By means of these various provisions it is the expectation of Fourierists that the personal inducements to exertion for the public interest, instead of being taken away, would be made much greater than at present, since every increase of the service rendered would be much more certain of leading to increase of reward than it is now, when accidents of position have so much influence. The efficiency of labor, they therefore expect, would be unexampled, while the saving of labor would be prodigious, by diverting to useful occupations that which is now wasted on things useless or hurtful, and by dispensing with the vast number of superfluous distributors, the buying and selling for the whole community being managed by a single agency. The free choice of individuals as to their manner of life would be no further interfered with than would be necessary for gaining the full advantages of co-operation in the industrial operations. Altogether, the picture of a Fourierist community is both attractive in itself and requires less from common humanity than any other known system of Socialism; and it is much to be desired that the scheme should have that fair trial which alone can test the workableness of any new scheme of social life.

The result of our review of the various difficulties of Socialism has led us to the conclusion that the various schemes for managing the productive resources of the country by public instead of private agency have a case for a trial, and some of them may eventually establish their claims to preference over the existing order of things, but that they are at present workable only by the élite of mankind, and have yet to prove their power of training mankind at large to the state of improvement which they presuppose. Far more, of course, may this be said of the more ambitious plan which aims at taking possession of the whole land and capital of the country, and beginning at once to administer it on the public account. Apart from all consideration of injustice to the present possessors, the very idea of conducting the whole industry of a country by direction from a single centre is so obviously chimerical, that nobody ventures to propose any mode in which it should be done; and it can hardly be doubted that if the revolutionary Socialists attained their immediate object, and actually had the whole property of the country at their disposal, they would find no other practicable mode of exercising their power over it than that of dividing it into portions, each to be made over to the administration of a small Socialist community. The problem of management, which we have seen to be so difficult even to a select population well prepared beforehand, would be thrown down to be solved as best it could by aggregations united only by locality, or taken indiscriminately from the population, including all the malefactors, all the idlest and most vicious, the most incapable of steady industry, forethought, or self-control, and a majority who, though not equally degraded, are yet, in the opinion of Socialists themselves as far as regards the qualities essential for the success of Socialism, profoundly demoralised by the existing state of society. It is saying but little to say that the introduction of Socialism under such conditions could have no effect but disastrous failure, and its apostles could have only the consolation that the order of society as it now exists would have perished first, and all who benefit by it would be involved in the common ruin—a consolation which to some of them would probably be real, for if appearances can be trusted the animating principle of too many of the revolutionary Socialists is hate; a very excusable hatred of existing evils, which would vent itself by putting an end to the present system at all costs even to those who suffer by it, in the hope that out of chaos would arise a better Kosmos, and in the impatience of desperation respecting any more gradual improvement. They are unaware that chaos is the very most unfavorable position for setting out in the construction of a Kosmos, and that many ages of conflict, violence, and tyrannical oppression of the weak by the strong must intervene; they know not that they would plunge mankind into the state of nature so forcibly described by Hobbes (Leviathan, Part I. ch. xiii.), where every man is enemy to every man:—

"In such condition there is no place for industry, because the fruit thereof is uncertain, and consequently no culture of the earth, no navigation, no use of the commodities that may be imported by sea, no commodious building, no instruments of moving and removing such things as require much force, no knowledge of the face of the earth, no account of time, no arts, no letters, no society; and, which is worst of all, continual fear and danger of violent death; and the life of man solitary, poor, nasty, brutish, and short."

If the poorest and most wretched members of a so-called civilised society are in as bad a condition as every one would be in that worst form of barbarism produced by the dissolution of civilised life, it does not follow that the way to raise them would be to reduce all others to the same miserable state. On the contrary, it is by the aid of the first who have risen that so many others have escaped from the general lot, and it is only by better organization of the same process that it may be hoped in time to succeed in raising the remainder.

THE IDEA OF PRIVATE PROPERTY
NOT FIXED BUT VARIABLE

The preceding considerations appear sufficient to show that an entire renovation of the social fabric, such as is contemplated by Socialism, establishing the economic constitution of society upon an entirely new basis, other than that of private property and competition, however valuable as an ideal, and even as a prophecy of ultimate possibilities, is not available as a present resource, since it requires from those who are to carry on the new order of things qualities both moral and intellectual, which require to be tested in all, and to be created in most; and this cannot be done by an Act of Parliament, but must be, on the most favorable supposition, a work of considerable time. For a long period to come the principle of individual property will be in possession of the field; and even if in any country a popular movement were to place Socialists at the head of a revolutionary government, in however many ways they might violate private property, the institution itself would survive, and would either be accepted by them or brought back by their expulsion, for the plain reason that people will not lose their hold of what is at present their sole reliance for subsistence and security until a substitute for it has been got into working order. Even those, if any, who had shared among themselves what was the property of others would desire to keep what they had acquired, and to give back to property in the new hands the sacredness which they had not recognised in the old.

But though, for these reasons, individual property has

presumably a long term before it, if only of provisional existence, we are not, therefore, to conclude that it must exist during that whole term unmodified, or that all the rights now regarded as appertaining to property belong to it inherently, and must endure while it endures. On the contrary, it is both the duty and the interest of those who derive the most direct benefit from the laws of property to give impartial consideration to all proposals for rendering those laws in any way less onerous to the majority. This, which would in any case be an obligation of justice, is an injunction of prudence also, in order to place themselves in the right against the attempts which are sure to be frequent to bring the Socialist forms of society prematurely into operation.

One of the mistakes oftenest committed, and which are the sources of the greatest practical errors in human affairs, is that of supposing that the same name always stands for the same aggregation of ideas. No word has been the subject of more of this kind of misunderstanding than the word property. It denotes in every state of society the largest powers of exclusive use or exclusive control over things (and sometimes, unfortunately, over persons) which the law accords, or which custom, in that state of society, recognizes; but these powers of exclusive use and control are very various, and differ greatly in different countries and in different states of society.

For instance, in early states of society, the right of property did not include the right of bequest. The power of disposing of property by will was in most countries of Europe a rather late institution; and long after it was introduced it continued to be limited in favor of what were called natural heirs. Where bequest is not permitted, individual property is only a life interest. And in fact, as

80

has been so well and fully set forth by Sir Henry Maine in his most instructive work on Ancient Law, the primitive idea of property was that it belonged to the family, not the individual. The head of the family had the management and was the person who really exercised the proprietary rights. As in other respects, so in this, he governed the family with nearly despotic power. But he was not free so to exercise his power as to defeat the co-proprietors of the other portions; he could not so dispose of the property as to deprive them of the joint enjoyment or of the succession. By the laws and customs of some nations the property could not be alienated without the consent of the male children; in other cases the child could by law demand a division of the property and the assignment to him of his share, as in the story of the Prodigal Son. If the association kept together after the death of the head, some other member of it, not always his son, but often the eldest of the family, the strongest, or the one selected by the rest, succeeded to the management and to the managing rights, all the others retaining theirs as before. If, on the other hand the body broke up into separate families, each of these took away with it a part of the property. I say the property, not the inheritance, because the process was a mere continuance of existing rights, not a creation of new; the manager's share alone lapsed to the association.

Then, again, in regard to proprietary rights over immovables (the principal kind of property in a rude age) these rights were of very varying extent and duration. By the Jewish law property in immovables was only a temporary concession; on the Sabbatical year it returned to the common stock to be redistributed; though we may surmise that in the historical times of the Jewish state this rule may have been successfully evaded. In many

81

countries of Asia, before European ideas intervened, nothing existed to which the expression property in land, as we understand the phrase, is strictly applicable. The ownership was broken up among several distinct parties, whose rights were determined rather by custom than by law. The government was part owner, having the right to a heavy rent. Ancient ideas and even ancient laws limited the government share to some particular fraction of the gross produce, but practically there was no fixed limit. The government might make over its share to an individual, who then became possessed of the right of collection and all the other rights of the state, but not those of any private person connected with the soil. These private rights were of various kinds. The actual cultivators or such of them as had been long settled on the land, had a right to retain possession; it was held unlawful to evict them while they paid the rent—a rent not in general fixed by agreement, but by the custom of the neighborhood. Between the actual cultivators and the state, or the substitute to whom the state had transferred its rights, there were intermediate persons with rights of various extent. There were officers of government who collected the state's share of the produce, sometimes for large districts, who, though bound to pay over to government all they collected, after deducting a percentage, were often hereditary officers. There were also, in many cases village communities, consisting of the reputed descendants of the first settlers of a village, who shared among themselves either the land or its produce according to rules established by custom, either cultivating it themselves or employing others to cultivate it for them, and whose rights in the land approached nearer to those of a landed proprietor, as understood in England, than those of any other party

82

concerned. But the proprietary right of the village was not individual, but collective; inalienable (the rights of individual sharers could only be sold or mortgaged with the consent of the community) and governed by fixed rules. In mediæval Europe almost all land was held from the sovereign on tenure of service, either military or agricultural; and in Great Britain even now, when the services as well as all the reserved rights of the sovereign have long since fallen into disuse or been commuted for taxation, the theory of the law does not acknowledge an absolute right of property in land in any individual; the fullest landed proprietor known to the law, the freeholder, is but a "tenant" of the Crown. In Russia, even when the cultivators of the soil were serfs of the landed proprietor, his proprietary right in the land was limited by rights of theirs belonging to them as a collective body managing its own affairs, and with which he could not interfere. And in most of the countries of continental Europe when serfage was abolished or went out of use, those who had cultivated the land as serfs remained in possession of rights as well as subject to obligations. The great land reforms of Stein and his successors in Prussia consisted in abolishing both the rights and the obligations, and dividing the land bodily between the proprietor and the peasant, instead of leaving each of them with a limited right over the whole. In other cases, as in Tuscany, the metayer farmer is virtually co-proprietor with the landlord, since custom, though not law, guarantees to him a permanent possession and half the gross produce, so long as he fulfils the customary conditions of his tenure.

Again: if rights of property over the same things are of different extent in different countries, so also are they exercised over different things. In all countries at a former time, and in some countries still, the right of property extended and extends to the ownership of human beings. There has often been property in public trusts, as in judicial offices, and a vast multitude of others in France before the Revolution; there are still a few patent offices in Great Britain, though I believe they will cease by operation of law on the death of the present holders; and we are only now abolishing property in army rank. Public bodies, constituted and endowed for public purposes, still claim the same inviolable right of property in their estates which individuals have in theirs, and though a sound political morality does not acknowledge this claim, the law supports it. We thus see that the right of property is differently interpreted, and held to be of different extent, in different times and places; that the conception entertained of it is a varying conception, has been frequently revised, and may admit of still further revision. It is also to be noticed that the revisions which it has hitherto undergone in the progress of society have generally been improvements. When, therefore, it is maintained, rightly or wrongly, that some change or modification in the powers exercised over things by the persons legally recognised as their proprietors would be beneficial to the public and conducive to the general improvement, it is no good answer to this merely to say that the proposed change conflicts with the idea of property. The idea of property is not some one thing, identical throughout history and incapable of alteration, but is variable like all other creations of the human mind; at any given time it is a brief expression denoting the rights over things conferred by the law or custom of some given society at that time; but neither on this point nor on any other has the law and custom of a given time and place a claim to be stereotyped for ever. A proposed reform in laws or customs is not necessarily objectionable because its adoption would imply, not the adaptation of all human affairs to the existing idea of property, but the adaptation of existing ideas of property to the growth and improvement of human affairs. This is said without prejudice to the equitable claim of proprietors to be compensated by the state for such legal rights of a proprietary nature as they may be dispossessed of for the public advantage. That equitable claim, the grounds and the just limits of it, are a subject by itself, and as such will be discussed hereafter. Under this condition, however, society is fully entitled to abrogate or alter any particular right of property which on sufficient consideration it judges to stand in the way of the public good. And assuredly the terrible case which, as we saw in a former chapter, Socialists are able to make out against the present economic order of society, demands a full consideration of all means by which the institution may have a chance of being made to work in a manner more beneficial to that large portion of society which at present enjoys the least share of its direct benefits.

Manufactured by Amazon.ca
Bolton, ON

34009078R00055